YOU CHOOSE
BOOKS™

Chinese Immigrants in America

An Interactive History Adventure

by Kelley Hunsicker

Consultant:
Jane Cheung, Museum Educator
Chinese American Museum
Los Angeles, California

Capstone
press®

Mankato, Minnesota

You Choose Books are published by Capstone Press,
151 Good Counsel Drive, P.O. Box 669, Mankato, Minnesota 56002.
www.capstonepress.com

Library of Congress Cataloging-in-Publication Data
Hunsicker, Kelley.
    Chinese immigrants in America : an interactive history adventure / by Kelley Hunsicker.
    p. cm. — (You choose books)
    Includes bibliographical references and index.
    ISBN-13: 978-1-4296-1355-2 (hardcover) ISBN-13: 978-1-4296-1762-8 (softcover pbk.)
    ISBN-10: 1-4296-1355-6 (hardcover) ISBN-10: 1-4296-1762-4 (softcover pbk.)
    1. Chinese Americans — History — 19th century — Juvenile literature. 2. Immigrants —
United States — History — 19th century — Juvenile literature. I. Title. II. Series.
E184.C5H87 2008
973'.0495109'034 — dc22   2007033715
Summary: Describes the experiences of Chinese immigrants upon arriving in the United States
in 1850. The reader's choices reveal historical details from the perspective of Chinese immigrants
who mine for gold, work on the Transcontinental Railroad, or settle in San Francisco's Chinatown.

Editorial Credits
Angie Kaelberer, editor; Julie Peters, set designer; Gene Bentdahl, book designer,
    Danielle Ceminsky, illustrator; Wanda Winch, photo researcher

Photo credits
Bancroft Library, University of California, Berkeley, 1905.04663-05242:04957, 57, 1905.17500
v.29:99-ALB, 105, 1963.002.1321-FR, 33, 1963.002:0280:-FR, 40, 19xx.111:03-PIC, 39;
Bridgeman Art Library International/Private Collection, Peter Newark American Pictures/
Chinese workers helping construct the Central Pacific Railroad, completed 1869 (colour
litho), American School, (19th century), 81; California Historical Society, (FN-01002), 10,
(FN-04470), 16, (FN-19651), 69, (FN-32819), cover, (FN-32830), 60; Collection of the
Oakland Museum of California, Gift of the Women's Board, George Henry Burgess, *San
Francisco in July, 1849-* detail, 1891, oil on canvas, 62" x 132.75", 70; Corbis, 64, 74; Corbis/
Bettmann, 85; Courtesy of the California History Room, California State Library, Sacramento,
California, 87; Getty Images Inc./Time Life Pictures/Mansell, 63; Granger Collection, New
York, 15, 47, 53; Image Works/HIP/NMPFT, 6; Image Works/Topham, 90; Mary Evans
Picture Library, 35; North Wind Picture Archives, 21, 95, 100; SuperStock, Inc., 99

1 2 3 4 5 6 13 12 11 10 09 08

The author dedicates this book to her mother, Mary Lou Rohn, for sharing her passion to
write, and to her father, Jerry Coone, for sharing his love of history.

TABLE OF CONTENTS

ABOUT YOUR ADVENTURE

YOU are an immigrant from China, leaving your family and village behind for a new life in the United States. You want to earn enough money to return to China and be wealthy the rest of your life. Will you succeed?

In this book, you'll explore how the choices people made meant the difference between life and death. The events you'll experience happened to real people.

Chapter One sets the scene. Then you choose which path to read. Follow the directions at the bottom of each page. The choices you make will change your outcome. After you finish one path, go back and read the others for new perspectives and more adventures.

*YOU CHOOSE the path
you take through history.*

In the 1850s, many people fled poverty in China for the promise of a better life in the United States.

Gold Mountain

Quick! You dive behind a tree as Qing government officials pass. Whew! They didn't see you. Tiptoeing to the road's edge, you see that all is clear. You continue making your way toward the coastal city of Canton.

It's 1850, and a civil war is raging in China. People are homeless and dying of hunger. Thousands are out of work.

This month, you couldn't pay the rent on your farm. Drought ruined your crops. Leaving China is illegal, but you believe it's the only way to make enough money to support your family.

You've heard rumors about a place in America called California. People call it Gold Mountain. They say gold covers the ground. You hope it's true, because you've sold your farm equipment to buy your ship ticket.

Many ships sit in Canton's harbor. Shipping laborers from China to America is a good way to make money. You find a captain and pay your $40 fare. You hope to make your fortune and return home soon.

You and at least 100 other Chinese men pack into the belly of the ship. Wooden bunks line the walls like rungs on a ladder. You claim one and lay your belongings there.

The six-week voyage seems endless. It's hot. The stench of human waste and body odor makes you feel sick.

The food served on the ship looks strange, and you are afraid to eat. You've only had a few bites since beginning the voyage. You're scared you won't live to reach Gold Mountain. Some passengers already have died. The ship's crew threw their bodies overboard.

Suddenly, you hear a cheer from the upper deck. Gold Mountain must be near. You will soon set foot in a new land filled with opportunity. If gold mining doesn't work out, there are always jobs in the shops and farms of San Francisco. And you don't know it now, but in 15 years, the U.S. government will build a transcontinental railroad. They will need many workers to complete it.

→ To mine gold in the 1850s, turn to page 9.

→ To stay in the city in the 1850s, turn to page 41.

→ To work on the railroad in the 1860s, turn to page 71.

Most Chinese immigrants arrived at the port city of San Francisco, California.

CHAPTER 2

Gold Fever!

As you step onto the gangplank, you squint. The bright sunlight makes it hard to see. The air smells salty and fresh.

A Chinese merchant meets you and your shipmates at the dock. He leads you to a part of town where other Chinese live. He tells you it's called Chinatown.

"You will need to buy a tent, food, and tin pans for mining," he explains.

The supplies are expensive. You decide to team up with six others from the ship.

"If we pool our money," you say, "we can buy extra supplies. We could use a mule, blankets, and a map."

Turn the page.

"What about one of these?" The merchant holds up a 'How to Mine' pamphlet written in Chinese. You take one.

"Stay together and keep away from white miners," the merchant warns before you leave. "If you don't, you'll be easy prey for bandits."

Many groups leave town together. Some eagerly head for the nearest river. Others walk farther inland. They want to avoid other miners and have a better chance to make a big gold strike. Where will you go?

✦ To go to the riverbeds, go to page 13.

✦ To travel inland to mine, turn to page 23.

Tents and small shacks dot the river's edge. "There's a clearing ahead," you say as you point to a spot between two Chinese camps. "We three can pitch the tent. You three gather firewood." With all of you working together, it takes only a couple of hours to set up camp.

"You know, it might be better if someone stays in camp to watch our belongings and to cook and clean," one of your partners says. "I will do that."

"That's a good idea. We'll combine the gold we find and share it equally," you reply.

Grabbing your tin pans, you and the others race to the water's edge. You bend and scoop a giant heap of mud and rocks. As you lift the pan out of the water, you swirl its contents. You remove the large rocks by hand.

Turn the page.

"No gold," you say, after peeking inside. You dig your pan in and begin again.

After many days of backbreaking labor, you find a few small nuggets.

"Gold! I found gold!" you yell, holding your nuggets high in the air and dancing in the shallow water. "Tonight, we'll celebrate." Instead of going to sleep early, you and your partners linger by the firelight.

A twig snaps at the edge of camp. In the darkness, you see the shadows of four men crouching in the underbrush.

Fearing for your lives, all of you flee into the woods. Food, blankets, and clothing fly into the air as the bandits search your belongings. When the noise stops, you return to camp.

"That was close," you say. "At least they didn't find our gold."

Most Chinese miners camped near each other for safety.

"What if they return? Maybe we should move," one of your partners answers.

"But if we move, that will mean giving up our claim to the gold here," you remind him.

15

"Let's sleep on it," he replies. At dawn the next morning, you all gather to make your decision.

❖ To move to a different location, turn to page **16**.

❖ To stay and continue mining, turn to page **18**.

The American River in California was a popular gold panning site for Chinese miners.

To avoid more trouble, you pack up and move. After walking many hours, you find a clearing near other Chinese camps. Again, you set up camp and begin panning for gold.

Suddenly, the shore clears of people. Miners begin packing their gear. You don't understand what is happening.

"Tax collectors! Tax collectors!" a Chinese man yells as he runs through your camp.

Now you understand. The miners are running away to avoid paying the Foreign Miners' Tax. The California state government passed a law that requires foreign-born workers to pay a tax of $3 each month. If you pay it, you won't be able to send any money to your family in China. What will you do?

↠ To stay and pay the taxes, turn to page 20.

↠ To run from the tax collectors, turn to page 29.

"Let's stay. I know there is more gold here. If we leave, we will lose it to someone else." Your partners agree.

Weeks pass without trouble. After another long day in the river, you and your partners combine your gold. Not bad! You have one thumb-size nugget and several smaller ones.

As you enter camp, you notice that the cook's forehead is bleeding. A stranger stands nearby. The end of his pistol is dripping blood.

Four more strangers circle behind you and your friends. "Where's your gold?" one growls.

You don't understand his words, but you know they want your gold. You remain silent.

The man behind you slams his pistol butt into your head, and you fall to the ground. The others do the same to your partners. The men begin searching your belongings.

"Here it is." One man grabs your bag holding today's gold. But that's all they find. After the first meeting with bandits, you learned to bury your gold just outside camp. Satisfied, the bandits leave.

You jump up to check on your friends. Everyone is okay. You are tidying up the camp when you hear shouting. Fearing more danger, you creep through the woods to explore.

"Tax collectors! The tax collectors are coming," warns a man from the other camp. "They are still several camps away. Run!"

You and your partners quickly talk it over. "We've just been robbed," you say. "Now a government man wants to take more of our gold. What should we do?"

→ To stay and pay taxes, turn to page **20**.

→ To flee the area to avoid paying taxes, turn to page **29**.

"I don't want trouble with the law," you say. "Let's pay the tax collector."

You go to your hiding place and quickly dig up some of the shiny nuggets. When the tax collector rides in, you pay him. He looks pleased and rides away.

You continue mining your claim. Gold isn't plentiful, but you find enough. You even send some nuggets to your family in China.

You keep mining for five years. But you never become rich. Another miner tells you of a large mining company that is hiring workers. "It's hard work," he says, "but steady pay."

You like the idea of steady pay. But if you leave, you may never strike it rich.

→ To work for the mining corporation, go to page 21.

→ To stay and continue mining here, turn to page 31.

Hydraulic mining was a good way to find gold, but it destroyed the land.

When gold was discovered, people thought it would last forever. But now, most of the surface gold has been mined. Companies are using water to mine ridges and hillsides. They call this work hydraulic mining. You like the idea of regular pay and decide to join them.

First, you help dig large ditches to redirect water from the river. These ditches feed into large pools. From there, hoses carry the water downhill to the mining area.

Turn the page.

The water picks up speed while traveling downhill, creating water pressure. This pressure blasts the earth. Dirt and rocks wash into a large trough called a sluice. The sluice separates sand from the rocks.

You pick through the rocks to find the gold nuggets. You then use a pan to separate the sand from the gold dust.

You find a lot of gold this way. But hydraulic mining destroys the land. Mountainsides slide down into the valleys, ruining the streams and land below.

After 10 years of mining, you've earned a nice amount of money. You have enough to open your own business or return to China a rich man.

➤ To open a business, turn to page 26.

➤ To return to China, turn to page 35.

You decide to travel inland. Camping near streams and riverbeds, you spend a few days panning for gold. Then you move on. You travel through California and north into the Rocky Mountains of Oregon Territory.

One day, you and your partners hear horses approaching. You all scramble into the brush.

Men with dark skin and long braids ride toward your camp. You watch from the trees. "What kind of men are these?" you whisper to your friends. "They're Indians — natives in this country," one answers.

The riders look tired and hungry. Should you offer them food and tea?

→ To offer them food and tea, turn to page 24.

→ To remain hidden, turn to page 34.

You leave your hiding place and return to camp. The riders look pitiful. You offer the first stranger a cup of warm tea.

The others dismount, gratefully taking the tea you are offering. Then you scoop bowls of cooked rice and offer them to the strangers. At first, they just stare at the food. Using hand motions, you urge them to eat. After finishing their meal, they ride away.

The next day, the riders return. They look inside your pan and see the shiny bits of gold.

They talk among themselves. Then, they lead you to a lake about 10 miles from camp.

As you walk out of the woods, you can't believe your eyes. The shoreline sparkles from gold. You pick up a fist-size nugget and take it back to show your partners.

You and your partners move your camp to the sparkling shoreline. You stay overnight, collecting as much gold as you can carry. You won't need to pan for gold anymore. You are rich.

Your load is heavy. The trip back to San Francisco will take at least a month. Now you must plan your future. You can return to your homeland a wealthy man. Or you can stay here, send for your family, and open a business of your own. What will you do?

→ To stay in San Francisco, turn to page **26**.

→ To return to China, turn to page **35**.

When you return to San Francisco, you notice big changes. When you arrived from China, people lived in tents and wooden shacks. Now, streets, sidewalks, and tall brick buildings fill the city.

Chinatown has grown too. You decide to stay, build a house, and open a business. But you haven't decided what business to start.

First, you buy a piece of land. You will build a home and then send for your family. You believe they will like this new land too.

While building your home, you find that many decorative objects you want to use cannot be found here. You send money to China to buy what you need. You wonder how many others have the same problem. Perhaps you could buy more than you need and open a curio shop in Chinatown.

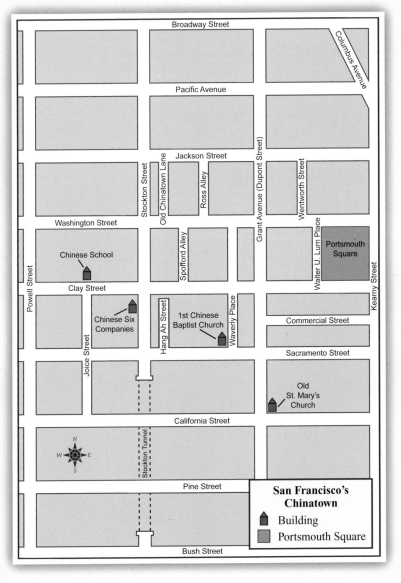

Broadway Street

Columbus Avenue

Pacific Avenue

Jackson Street

Stockton Street

Old Chinatown Lane

Ross Alley

Grant Avenue (Dupont Street)

Wentworth Street

Washington Street

Walter U. Lum Place

Portsmouth Square

Chinese School

Spofford Alley

Powell Street

Clay Street

Kearny Street

Chinese Six Companies

Hang Ah Street

1st Chinese Baptist Church

Waverly Place

Joice Street

Commercial Street

Sacramento Street

Old St. Mary's Church

California Street

N
W — E
S

Stockton Tunnel

Pine Street

San Francisco's Chinatown

■ Building

■ Portsmouth Square

Bush Street

Turn the page.

When you were mining in the wilderness, you missed the Chinese food you love. You also notice that many curious tourists visit Chinatown. They eat in the Chinese restaurants. A restaurant might also be a good business to open. You want your business to succeed. What do you decide?

➤ To open a curio shop, turn to page **36**.

➤ To open a restaurant, turn to page **37**.

You know that some tax collectors act like bandits. Even though they are paid a percentage of what they collect, they take more gold and keep it for themselves."

"Let's run," you say. "I don't want to give any more gold away." You and your partners hurry to escape.

After pitching camp for the night, you build a small fire to heat water for tea. While waiting for the water to boil, you wash and braid your hair. Long pigtails are law in China. All men must wear them. Because you plan to return home someday, you wear your hair in this traditional way.

Four men on horseback enter your camp. The three white men are tax collectors. The other is an American Indian working as a tracker for the tax collectors.

Turn the page.

"Where's your gold?" the tax collectors ask as they search your belongings.

"Well, lookie what we have here," one tax collector says, holding your bag of gold. "Now what should we do with all of you?"

"I say we kill them and take it all," one of his partners answers.

Before you can run, the three tax collectors pull out their guns and open fire. As you and your partners fall to the ground, you have one last thought of your family back in China. You'll never see them again.

THE END

To follow another path, turn to page 9.
To read the conclusion, turn to page 101.

You and your partners decide to stay where you are. You mine for years with little success, but you don't give up.

One day, you see something shining in the river. "Over here! Look what I found." You try to lift a large chunk of gold from the river bottom. "It must weigh 40 pounds," you shout.

The others stop mining. At first, everyone just stares at the golden rock. They help you lift it from the water, realizing you have just hit pay dirt. You will all be rich.

"We can't carry this large rock. Let's chisel it into tiny pieces," one partner says.

The next day, as you pack to leave, a gang of Mexican bandits rides into your camp. You try to run, but you can't. There are too many riders, and they are too fast.

Turn the page.

The bandits dismount and grab you and your partners by your braided hair. They use the ropelike braids to tie you together. No one can move without tugging the others along.

"Where's your gold?" the bandits demand.

You all remain silent.

The bandits begin beating you and your friends. Each blow increases your pain. Soon, you can't take it anymore.

"There," you point. "It's there."

You slump to the ground. Then you hear a click. You look up to see a pistol aimed in your direction. Boom! Everything goes black as you take your last breath.

You've just met Joaquin Murieta and his gang. They roam the countryside robbing and killing Chinese miners.

Joaquin Murieta led a group of outlaws believed to be guilty of robbing and killing miners.

In May 1853, California offers a $1,000 reward for Murieta's capture, dead or alive. Chinese businessmen contribute another $3,000. Murieta is killed a few months later by men eager to collect the bounty. Unfortunately, it is too late for you.

THE END

To follow another path, turn to page 9.
To read the conclusion, turn to page 101.

You remain hidden, watching from a safe distance as the riders search your belongings. When they leave, you return to camp. "Hurry, let's pack. We must leave before they return."

You never strike it rich. You never return to China. And you never have enough money to send to your family.

In hopelessness and shame, you continue your wandering lifestyle. You barely earn enough to live. Years later, you die penniless in this strange country.

THE END

To follow another path, turn to page 9.
To read the conclusion, turn to page 101.

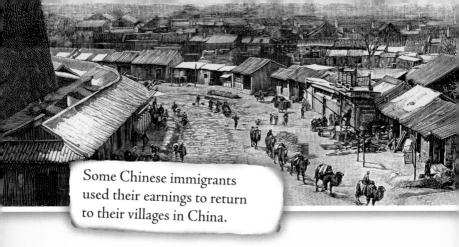

Some Chinese immigrants used their earnings to return to their villages in China.

You return to your village in China and buy a large piece of land. On the land, you build a comfortable home.

You gather your relatives together. "I want to share my good fortune," you tell them. They all move in with you. Your wealth brings you respect in the village. This life would not be possible without the gold you found in San Francisco.

THE END

To follow another path, turn to page 9.
To read the conclusion, turn to page 101.

You find a building in Chinatown on Dupont Street. There's a restaurant on one side and a cigar shop on the other.

You hire Chinese workers to put in a large picture window. In the window, you display the vases, statues, and other decorations for sale. You paint the building bright yellow and hang red paper lanterns near the doorway. Using Chinese letters, you paint a red and gold sign to hang in front of your new shop. Soon, you will open for business.

THE END

To follow another path, turn to page 9.
To read the conclusion, turn to page 101.

You find a large three-story building on Jackson Street. It will make a fine restaurant.

You remodel the inside and paint the walls red. All day, a crew of men lug furniture and crates and heap them just outside your door.

One worker enters and hands you the bill. "Where do you want us to put this stuff?"

"Bring all the nicest tables up to the third floor," you say. Next, the workers carry up the matching chairs and stools.

"These are fine," a worker says, rubbing the back of a chair. "You can't find furniture built this well here."

"I have linens, pillows, and ornaments that will decorate this floor too," you say. "The third floor will be for my very important guests."

Turn the page.

Next, you show the workers the tables, chairs, and decorations that go on the second floor. "The taller tables go on the balconies," you say. Each balcony is transformed into an elegant dining area.

"What goes in here?" A worker points to a small room off the first floor.

"Put the two small tables and lamps in here. Then take all those pillows and neatly toss them around on the floor. This area is where gentlemen diners will relax after dinner."

38

One last small crate catches your attention. Carefully, you carry it to a small room near the front of your restaurant. You open the box and pull out a statue. "This is for good luck." You place the statue on a pedestal that sits in the center of the room.

Elegant Chinese restaurants were popular with both San Francisco natives and tourists.

You paint the outside of your building red, yellow, green, and orange. You hang brightly colored lanterns from the balconies. Once you open, your restaurant quickly becomes one of the most successful in Chinatown.

THE END

To follow another path, turn to page 9.
To read the conclusion, turn to page 101.

San Francisco's Chinatown was influenced by the art and architecture of China.

CHAPTER 3

Chinatown

As you step off the ship, you walk through blocks of half-finished buildings. The sound of hammers echoes in the air.

You turn onto Dupont Street. It looks almost like home. Chinese men in baggy knee-high pants, loose-fitting blue quilted pullovers, and long braided pigtails fill the streets. The pigtails are law in China. All men must wear them. Like you, most Chinese men in the United States plan to return to China someday. Wearing the traditional hairstyle is a sign you'll be welcomed back.

Colorful paper lanterns sway overhead. Thin banners of red cloth with gold Chinese lettering hang from each building.

Turn the page.

You notice the smell of familiar food in the air. Suddenly, you realize that you're very hungry. You stop in at a restaurant. The owner, Cheng, comes out to take your order.

"What is this part of the city called?" you ask him.

"Are you joking?" Cheng answers. "This is Chinatown." No wonder you feel at home here.

As Cheng serves you hot tea and rice, he asks about your plans. "I'm here to make my fortune — maybe in the gold fields," you reply.

"Everyone who comes to this new land hopes to find gold. But gold is not as plentiful anymore. Mining camps can be a dangerous place for Chinese men. White men who can't find gold often take their frustrations out on the Chinese miners. You might want to consider staying here."

Cheng tells you about the jobs available in San Francisco. "Employers pay good wages," he says. "And if you have money, you can even open your own business." But first, he suggests learning more about Americans and their ways.

You're not sure what to do. The idea of opening a business interests you. It's something you could never afford to do in China.

You do have a little money. But maybe it will be smarter to wait. The high wages sound good too. And by taking a job, you'll be able to learn the customs here and save more money. What will you do?

➤ To work and save money, turn to page 44.

➤ To open a small business, turn to page 52.

You decide to work and save more money. But first, you need to find a place to stay.

"There's a boardinghouse nearby," Cheng tells you.

When you get there, you learn that the owner has a bed available. You climb a narrow stairway and walk to the end of the hall.

In the tiny room, cots are everywhere. They line the floors and are attached to the walls, just like in the ship. Five of the cots are occupied by Chinese men. The men look sick.

"Where do I sleep?" you ask.

The owner points to an empty cot in the far corner. Throwing your belongings on one end, you plop onto the mattress to sleep.

The next day, you return to Cheng's restaurant to ask him about jobs.

"Where can I find work?" you ask.

"Let's see." Cheng scratches his head. "Senator William Gwin needs a house servant — no experience necessary," he says. That's good, because you don't have any.

Then he adds, "Mr. George Peck, a produce merchant, needs laborers for his fields."

You do have experience in farming. Which job will you take?

→ To work for Senator Gwin, turn to page **46**.

→ To farm with Mr. Peck, turn to page **49**.

You decide to work for Senator Gwin. When you arrive at the house, a friendly white woman answers the door.

"Are you here about the job?" she asks, motioning for you to enter.

Amazed by the space inside, you wonder why one family would need so much room. In China, several families would live in this space.

"My name is Mrs. Gwin," she says.

You try to repeat her name, but it doesn't come out exactly like she says it. Then, you tell her your name.

"I'll call you John," she says. Many people here call Chinese men "John."

She grabs a broom and begins sweeping the floor. Then she hands it to you. You copy her. She nods and smiles her approval.

William Gwin served as a
U.S. senator for nine years.

After you complete a task, she teaches you
a new one. Before long, you understand what
she wants.

While working at Senator Gwin's house,
you learn to speak a little English. Even
though your English is not good, it is enough
to communicate.

You like working here, but you want to make more money. You are earning $5 per week. This salary is much more than you could earn in China. But in San Francisco, $5 is a small sum. Mr. Gwin doesn't want to pay more. You think it's time to move on.

You could try farming. But you don't know much about the fruits and vegetables grown here. You wonder if Mr. Peck still needs help. He could teach you.

Or with your housekeeping skills, you could work for one of the fancy hotels in town. What will you do?

➤ To look for Mr. Peck, turn to page 51.

➤ To work for a hotel, turn to page 60.

48

Cheng takes you to the produce market to meet Mr. Peck.

"Do you still need laborers to work on your farm?" Cheng asks.

"We can always use another pair of hands," Mr. Peck replies.

Cheng leaves you with Mr. Peck. He takes you to his farm, just outside San Francisco.

You share a tent near the fields with several other Chinese men. Each day, you work many hours in the fields. You learn to grow potatoes, cabbage, and turnips.

Working in the fields isn't a perfect life. Mosquitoes and fleas bite your skin. Rats sometimes visit your tent. But because you're earning $8 a week, you don't complain.

Turn the page.

You spend four years working for Mr. Peck. One day, he stops by the tents.

"I'm sorry, but I'm going to sell the farm," he tells you and the other workers. "This new state needs schools. I'm going to build one in Sacramento."

You're sorry to hear Mr. Peck's news. He's been a good boss. You aren't sure what you want to do next.

With the money you've saved, you can return to San Francisco and buy a small piece of land to farm. But you would also like to see more of this country. You could buy food and tools and work your way across the land. What will you do?

➤ To buy land to farm, turn to page 62.

➤ To work across America, turn to page 64.

You return to the produce market, but can't find Mr. Peck.

"He quit farming to open a school," says a man at a produce stand.

You see another man hiring laborers to make farmland where the Sacramento and San Joaquin rivers meet. You are not sure what to do. This job isn't what you had in mind when you left Senator Gwin's house. If the Gwins haven't hired anyone yet, maybe you could return. What will you do?

→ To work on farmland, turn to page 57.

→ To return to Senator Gwin's, turn to page 59.

You rent a bed at a local boardinghouse and rest a few days. You learn that American men don't wash clothes. They consider it women's work, and women are scarce in California.

Miners pay a small fortune to ship their dirty clothes about 2,500 miles across the Pacific Ocean to the Sandwich Islands. There, the clothes are washed and shipped back. A laundry might be a good business to open here.

You rent a shack near Washerwoman's Bay, just outside San Francisco. You charge $5 for 12 shirts. Customers come as your good reputation spreads. You replace the shack with a better building and live in the back.

One day, three fierce-looking white men enter your laundry. "Give us those shirts," one demands, pointing at a stack of freshly ironed shirts.

Many Chinese immigrants found success by starting laundry businesses.

"Claim ticket, please," you say.

They don't have a claim ticket. You know you have no shirts that belong to them.

If you give them the shirts, they may go away. But what will you tell the real owner? If you don't give them the shirts, they could cause trouble. What will you do?

→ To give the shirts to the men, turn to page 54.

→ To refuse to give the shirts to the men, turn to page 56.

"Sorry," you say, bowing slightly. "I'll wrap the shirts for you."

You tie the clean shirts with string and hand them to the men. They laugh as they walk out the door.

The next day, a customer enters your shop and hands you a claim ticket.

"I'm very sorry," you say. "I don't have your shirts."

"What do you mean? I left them here a couple days ago."

"I'm sorry. Three men came in and stole them."

The man slams his fist on the tabletop. "Then you will give me $20 for each shirt they stole."

"That price is too high," you say. "The shirts were worn and patched. I'll give you $20 for all of them."

"We'll see what the law has to say about this. I'll see you in court," he says.

In California, Chinese have no rights in court. The judge finds in favor of the customer. You must pay the high price he demands.

Your business is doing well. Until now, you've felt safe. But how long will you remain safe? Perhaps you should leave and begin again somewhere else. What will you do?

→ To move somewhere else, turn to page 67.

→ To stay, turn to page 68.

The shirts do not belong to the men. You refuse to hand them over. You want to protect your customer's belongings.

The men become angry. They beat you. Then they trash your shop, steal your cash, and take the shirts. You lie on the floor, bruised and in pain.

You report the robbery to the police, even though you know they will do nothing. The police aren't interested in protecting Chinese people.

You decide it's too risky to stay here any longer. You pack your belongings and leave.

⟿ *Turn to page* **67**.

You sign on and climb into the wagon. Your new job is in a swamp swarming with mosquitoes. Wading into knee-deep water, you cut and remove rotted plants. The work goes slowly. You can't use horses to haul the loads. Their hooves sink too deep into the mud.

You work long, tiresome days. Then another Chinese laborer invents shoes for the horses. He weaves them from the tall tule grass that grows in the marsh. The shoes give the horses better traction in the mud.

Growing lettuce and other vegetable crops was hot, punishing work.

Turn the page.

After clearing the vegetation in one area, you begin building a series of gates, ditches, and dams. These barriers will help control the water levels.

But one day, a flood of water rushes in. The wooden gates snap like twigs. You fight the current, grabbing anything you can get your hands on. Covered in mud, you finally manage to make your way to shore. Others are not as fortunate. They drown in the deep river.

After your close call, you decide to quit the job. A local farmer offers you a job. You continue farming until you save enough money to return to San Francisco. You hope to soon save enough money to send for your family.

THE END

To follow another path, turn to page 9.
To read the conclusion, turn to page 101.

You return to Senator Gwin's house. You hope they have not hired anyone else yet.

"John! You're back." Mrs. Gwin's smile tells you she is happy to see you. She hasn't yet found a replacement for you. Besides, she likes how clean you keep her house.

You continue working at the Gwins until 1855, when Mr. Gwin loses his senate seat. You decide to return to China. You and your family live a good life with the money you earned in America.

THE END

To follow another path, turn to page 9.
To read the conclusion, turn to page 101.

Chinese workers found jobs in fine hotels and restaurants in San Francisco.

You take a job as a chamber servant at the Tremont Hotel. You clean rooms, send out laundry, and take care of sick guests.

One Sunday morning, a fire starts in a building across the street. The guests panic. Windows break as the guests throw their trunks out into the street.

"John! Gather all the blankets and drench them in water," the hotel owner orders. "Nail them to the side of the building facing the fire."

You find a ladder, a hammer, and some nails. Some guests volunteer to help. Together, you cover the wall with the wet blankets.

Climbing to the roof, you begin pouring barrels of water onto the building. Others move beds and furniture outside.

The roof catches fire several times, but you kill the flames. The fire dies. The hotel is safe.

Eventually, a fire does burn the Tremont Hotel to the ground. But by that time, you've saved enough money to buy a small house. You continue working in hotels and sending money to your family in China. One day, you hope they will join you in America.

THE END

To follow another path, turn to page 9.
To read the conclusion, turn to page 101.

You buy a small plot of land just outside the city. You see another Chinese farmer working his land.

"Hello," you say. "What type of vegetables do you grow?"

"I grow potatoes and cabbage," he says. "But almost any type of crop grows well here."

You divide your land into three sections. Then, you buy supplies to plant string beans, cabbage, and strawberries. After the first harvest, you take them to the market.

During the week, you work your land. On weekends, you pick the newly ripened produce and return to the market.

You sell quality produce and do well in this new land. You work hard and eventually have enough money to buy a small home.

Chinese farmers sold their vegetables and fruits at produce stands in the cities.

You hope to one day earn enough to send for your family in China. Sadly, that day never comes. You live the rest of your life alone, farming your land and selling your vegetables.

THE END

To follow another path, turn to page 9.
To read the conclusion, turn to page 101.

After the Civil War, Chinese workers found jobs at southern sugar and cotton plantations.

During the next 15 years, you move from town to town, working at whatever job you can find. As you move toward the southern states, you pass burned homes, fields, and towns. You learn they were destroyed during the country's Civil War.

Before the war, African American slaves worked in the plantation fields. But now, the South is going through something called Reconstruction. Without slaves, landowners need help.

You sign a contract to work in a cotton field in Mississippi. The landowner, Mr. Greenley, promises $20 a month.

Mr. Greenley's foreman makes you work many hours each day in the fields. You have little water and even less food. The foreman whips sick and weak workers to force them to work faster. He even shoots one worker who protests the treatment. You know you have to get out of your contract.

One day, you sneak into town and stop in a lawyer's office. "What do you want?" the lawyer asks.

You tell him about the working conditions and abuse. The landowner is not living up to the contract you signed. The lawyer doesn't say anything for a long time.

Turn the page.

"Well, since the end of the war, you Chinese probably have more rights here than any other place in the United States," he finally says. "The Reconstructionists don't want Chinese slaves to replace black slaves. I'll take your case."

You go to court, and the judge decides in your favor. You're free of your contract. You decide to move to Louisiana. With the money you've saved, you open a small grocery store in New Orleans. When business becomes steady, you send money to your family in China. You plan for them to join you soon.

THE END

To follow another path, turn to page 9.
To read the conclusion, turn to page 101.

You walk through the wilderness, looking for another town. You see crews of men working for the railroad. They look tired and dirty. The men have no one to wash their clothes. This might be a good place to settle.

You set up camp near a small river and nail your sign to a tree. Soon, you have more business than you can handle. When the workers move to a new location, you follow.

After a few years, you grow tired of moving from place to place. You settle in Rock Springs, Wyoming. With the money you've saved, you buy a small piece of land and build a house. The front of your house serves as the laundry. You live in the back. Someday, you hope to send for your family.

THE END

To follow another path, turn to page 9.
To read the conclusion, turn to page 101.

You have many customers and a good reputation among them. You decide to stay. After all, this is the first time you've had any trouble. You pay the steep price to replace the stolen shirts.

Your business grows, but most Chinese aren't as lucky as you are. As more unsuccessful miners pour into San Francisco, jobs become scarce. Many business owners prefer hiring Chinese workers, because the Chinese will work for lower wages than white workers. This enrages the white workers. They pressure business owners to stop hiring Chinese workers.

The night of July 23, 1877, a meeting of white workers turns violent. The mob roams the streets in San Francisco. The white men beat Chinese workers and burn Chinese-owned businesses.

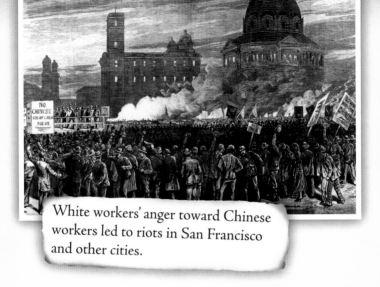

White workers' anger toward Chinese workers led to riots in San Francisco and other cities.

You awake in the middle of the night to the smell of smoke. Leaping from your bed, you run to the front of your house. The laundry area is on fire!

Grabbing a blanket, you beat at the flames. The fire spreads too fast. You run outside and watch helplessly as everything you own burns to ashes.

THE END

To follow another path, turn to page 9.
To read the conclusion, turn to page 101.

San Francisco's population grew from 500 people in 1848 to 25,000 in 1850.

CHAPTER 4

The Impossible Task

You gather your few possessions and leave the ship. As you stand on the dock, you wonder which way to go. You turn around and bump into another Chinese man.

"Be careful!" he says sternly. Seeing the confused look on your face, his voice becomes kinder. "Are you just off the ship?" You nod. "Come with me to Chinatown, then," the man replies.

On the way, you learn the man's name is Wong. He takes you inside his store and gives you hot tea and rice. Then he tells you about this new land.

Turn the page.

"Gold has become scarcer than it once was. Mining can be dangerous for a Chinese man," he explains. "But there are lots of places to work here."

You decide to find a job in San Francisco. Wong tells you about a nearby boardinghouse, and you rent a room there. You find a job with the city, building streets and bridges. Then you hear the Central Pacific Railroad wants to hire Chinese laborers. They pay $28 each month. This sum is more than you have ever earned. You sign on.

Three wagons sit nearby, all heading for different worksites. Where will you go?

➤ To work in the flatlands outside Sacramento, turn to page 73.

➤ To work at Cape Horn, turn to page 75.

➤ To work at Summit Tunnel, turn to page 79.

As you travel to the Chinese camp, white railroad workers glare and yell insults at you. You will work for lower wages, so they believe you're taking jobs away from them.

The white workers look huge and dirty to you. Because you are shorter and thinner than they are, they think you're not strong enough for the job. You decide to prove them wrong.

You settle in and see the supervisor. He assigns you a job. You begin work right away.

Using a pickax, you begin pounding the dusty ground. You dig out rocks to make the ground level. In some places, you scoop out carts of dirt. In other places, you fill holes with dirt. Then you pound the earth to form a flat surface. The other crews will then lay the rails across this newly graded land.

Turn the page.

The land had to be graded until it was level before workers could build the railroad tracks.

You work steadily, not even stopping to wipe the sweat from your brow. At the day's end, your crew has prepared more ground than the white crews have. "Great job!" says your supervisor.

The boss wants some of the crewmembers to move to a new location to begin chopping trees. The others will stay here and keep grading land. What will you do?

⋆ To move to the new location, turn to page 76.

⋆ To stay and continue grading, turn to page 92.

Your wagon reaches the foothills of the Sierra Nevada mountain range. Massive redwoods and pines grow everywhere. Some of the trunks are 8 feet wide. Crews must remove them to lay tracks.

Beyond the giant trees is a ridge of solid rock nicknamed Cape Horn. You will need to blast a roadbed on the mountainside, which is 1,332 feet above the American River.

The task seems impossible, but new crews arrive each day to help. Some clear the giant trees, while others begin work on Cape Horn. Where will you work?

↠ To clear the giant trees, turn to page 76.

↠ To blast the roadbed at Cape Horn, turn to page 77.

Removing the huge trees is not easy. Some stand more than 100 feet tall. After a tree falls, you put blasting powder around the stump to loosen it. Rocks and bits of wood fly through the air. Men run from the tiny missiles.

You work long days to clear the rocks and trees. Then you grade the cleared surface, preparing it for tracks.

Once the work is done here, you must move on. You can work at Cape Horn or move to the Summit Tunnel. Which will you choose?

➤ To begin working on Cape Horn, go to page 77.

➤ To move to Summit Tunnel, turn to page 79.

Cape Horn is untouched. No trails run through it. Cutting a roadbed won't be easy.

Instead of tunneling through the mountain, the rails will climb the outside, circling the mountainside. To make the flat surface for the tracks, part of the mountain must go.

You watch as white crews try to blast the mountainside. The white workers aren't sure-footed. You think it's because of their size.

"We are smaller than the men working on the mountainside," you tell the supervisor. "We can do a better job." He agrees to let you try.

Your fellow workers tie a rope around your waist. They hold the other end as they lower you down the cliff. You use a small hand drill to bore into the rock. You pack the hole with explosive powder, add a fuse, and light it.

Turn the page.

"Lift me up!" you yell.

Quickly, the men pull the rope, taking you out of harm's way. After the explosion, you go down again to make another hole for the blasting powder.

The railroad plans to blast tunnels through the Sierra Nevada mountain range. They want the help of experienced blasters. Will you go to the mountains or stay to complete the work at Cape Horn?

➤ To move to Summit Tunnel, go to page 79.

➤ To stay at Cape Horn, turn to page 94.

The railroad needs to blast 13 tunnels through the mountain. Six lie in a 2-mile stretch. You will work on the longest. Tunnel Number 6, the Summit Tunnel, will stretch 1,659 feet through the mountainside.

"We're going to start working around the clock," says Chief Engineer Samuel Montague. The white workers are divided into three eight-hour shifts. But the Chinese men work a 12-hour day or night shift.

You work in three-man crews. You hold the rock drill. The two other men swing 18-pound sledgehammers.

The solid granite mountainside remains stubborn. Even with your combined efforts, you only manage to move 6 to 12 inches of rock each day.

Turn the page.

"I'm not satisfied with the progress," says Montague. "We're going to divide into two crews. One will work here, and one will work on the other side of the mountain. Both teams will work toward the center."

Then Montague thinks this pace still won't be fast enough. "We're going to send a crew to the top of the mountain too," he says.

These men will dig hundreds of feet into the rock until they reach the tunnel elevation. When they reach their destination, the crews will blast toward the outside of the tunnel. This way, crews will be on both sides of the summit, blasting toward the center. Plus, there will be two crews working from inside the summit, blasting outward. The work should move ahead four times as fast. Where will you work?

The dynamite used to blast tunnels through solid rock sometimes proved deadly.

To work from outside toward the center, turn to page **82**.

To work from inside toward the outside, turn to page **83**.

You work with a crew of 12 men. One crewmember is the leader. He talks with the boss and tells you what to do. Another crewmember cooks all your meals. You pool your money to buy food. The railroad brings in fish, fruit, bamboo shoots, seaweed, and mushrooms from San Francisco.

Each day, you do whatever task needs doing. You drill, blast, shovel, and haul pieces of granite away from the tunnel entrance. And each day, you inch closer toward the center.

Unexpectedly, a worker dies from a blast during the night. Because the day shift has more help, the supervisor wants a replacement. Will you move to nights or remain on days?

→ To move to the night shift, turn to page 85.

→ To remain on the day shift, turn to page 95.

You climb to the mountaintop and begin blasting. You remove the loosened chunks of granite. Then you place timbers inside to keep the mountainside from caving in. This job takes too much time.

The bosses have a plan to quickly remove the blasted rock. Loading the granite pieces into a train locomotive would make it easy to remove tons of rock.

But how will they get the locomotive up the mountainside? Horses are strong but not sure-footed on rocky ledges. Mules and oxen are, though. The bosses need to find a man experienced in handling these beasts. The bosses hire the best muleskinner they can find, Missouri Bill. He uses five pairs of oxen to pull the heavy car. It takes six weeks, but he finally brings the locomotive to the top.

Turn the page.

Meanwhile, you help construct a 50-foot building to house the locomotive. When the locomotive arrives, you help move it into the building. The locomotive hauls granite from inside the mountain. It also lowers timbers into the tunnel shaft. The work goes faster. You clear a foot of tunnel each day.

In December, you finally reach the center and can begin blasting in both directions. Montague wants his crews to work 24-hour days. He needs volunteers to work the night shift. Which shift will you work?

To move to the night shift, go to page **85**.

To remain on the day shift, turn to page **95**.

Chinese railroad workers were known for their neat, orderly camps.

The days are hot and humid. You choose to work the night shift. The night temperatures are more comfortable.

All too soon, winter arrives in full force. Wooden shacks replace the workers' tents. In all, 44 storms hit the mountains.

Turn the page.

The snow piles higher with each new storm. You dig tunnels beneath the snow to get to the worksite each night. You carry a lantern to find your way. Sometimes, the snow tunnels cave in. You dig new ones and continue to work.

When spring comes, you repair bridges, dams, and trestles damaged by the snow. Crews continue to work through the mountains.

Another year passes. About 8,000 Chinese men work on the summit. Another 3,000 Chinese are moving ahead to begin laying track in the desert. Where will you work?

➤ To continue working in the mountains, go to page 87.

➤ To advance to the desert, turn to page 91.

Charles Crocker supported hiring Chinese workers, but became angry at their strike.

Charles Crocker wants to hire more Chinese workers. But other companies want them too. The labor force grows scarce. The railroad increases wages to $35 a month. But Chinese workers are still working 12-hour shifts each day.

On June 25, 1867, the entire Chinese workforce goes on strike. "We want $40 a month and to work an eight-hour day, like you promised," you say.

Turn the page.

The Central Pacific doesn't want to pay higher wages. Instead, they send men south to hire 5,000 newly freed slaves. The men find no takers. Meanwhile, you and the other strikers stay in camp, careful not to cause trouble.

Crocker cuts off the strikers' food supply. You and your friends grow weak from hunger. On July 1, Crocker approaches.

"Look, you don't make the rules," he says. "We do. The raise to $35 a month is more than fair. If you come back now, I'll forget about this strike. But if you don't, you won't receive any wages for the three weeks you worked in June."

You want to work, but the men leading the strike scare you. They threaten to whip anyone who returns to work. What will you do?

→ To return to work, go to page 89.

→ To obey the Chinese leaders, turn to page 90.

"I want to work again," you say to the others. Some agree, some don't.

"Otherwise, we worked three weeks in June for nothing," you remind them.

"What about our leaders? They have threatened anyone who goes back to work before Crocker gives in to our demands," one worker says.

Crocker promises protection to anyone who goes back to work. You return, even though Crocker didn't meet any of your demands. The crew moves into Nevada and then into Utah.

Turn to page 97.

Fearing the Chinese leaders, you wait until they say you can work again. But Crocker makes no more offers. The Chinese leaders finally give in, and you return to work. The railroad soon moves into Nevada. By 1869, you are working in Utah. It won't be long before the railroad is finished.

As the workers entered Utah, they knew the railroad was close to being finished.

Turn to page 97.

The trees of the Sierra Nevada range in California supply wood for building and fuel. Streams provide water. But in July 1868, you enter a Nevada desert. Only a few trees grow here. No streams flow. The railroad must ship food, water, and lumber through the desert.

You travel to Palisade Canyon with other crews. The rest of the workers follow. They bring water, railroad ties, and other supplies. Canvas tent towns spring up overnight. The next morning, they disappear as the crew works its way east.

To keep moving, the railroad sends supplies ahead to Promontory Summit. There, the tracks will join the Union Pacific's rails. The Transcontinental Railroad will finally be finished.

Turn to page 97.

Your success has forced the white crews to work harder. Charles Crocker, the supervisor, likes the competition. He gets more tracks laid each day. He likes how hard you work and gives you more responsibility.

You learn to blast the large boulders. This job requires three people. One holds an iron spike. The other two use a sledgehammer to pound a hole. Then, the crew fills the hole with blasting powder, lights the fuse, and runs.

The powder explodes, blasting away some of the rock. While others clear away the loosened rocks, you and your partners begin drilling another hole. You continue drilling until you blast the boulder into small pieces.

All day, you blast the large rocks. The sun begins to set. You have one more boulder to blast before quitting time.

As usual, you light the fuse and run. But this time, something goes wrong. The blast explodes quicker than usual. Instead of blasting the rock, it blasts out of the hole, toward you.

You fall to the ground without ever knowing what happened. You are just one of many railroad workers who will lose their lives in blasting accidents.

THE END

To follow another path, turn to page 9.
To read the conclusion, turn to page 101.

Your crew works beside you, like tiny spiders climbing up and down the massive mountainside. Some do not get out of the way fast enough. The exploding rock kills them. Others take their place, and the work continues.

One day, when you're being lowered to drill another hole, the rope slips. You fall into the American River far below. You are one of the many who lose their lives while building the Transcontinental Railroad.

THE END

To follow another path, turn to page 9.
To read the conclusion, turn to page 101.

The winter of 1866 tested the railroad workers' strength.

You like working by daylight. You decide to remain on the day shift.

The heat drains your strength, so you are happy when the weather turns cooler. You build a wooden shack to replace your tent. Soon, the snow begins. Snowstorms during the winter of 1866–1867 drop 40 feet of snow on the mountains.

Turn the page.

Howling winds form snowdrifts 80 feet high. In order to continue work, you dig a maze of tunnels beneath the snow. Traveling by lantern light, you move through the tunnels from your shack to the workplace and back.

The snow causes problems. Avalanches occur often, destroying everything in their paths. One day as you are blasting, you hear a sound like thunder. Each second, the noise of the avalanche grows louder. It is the last sound you ever hear.

Your body remains covered with ice and snow until the spring thaw. You are just one of the many workers who dies during that harsh winter.

THE END

To follow another path, turn to page 9.
To read the conclusion, turn to page 101.

By March 30, 1869, the Central Pacific has only about 75 miles of track to complete.

"I bet you that my crew can lay more track in a single day than your crew can," boasts Charles Crocker. He is proud of the work you and the other Chinese workers have done. He wants to prove the Central Pacific crew is better than the Union Pacific crew.

"I'll take that bet," says Thomas Durant of the Union Pacific. "Let's make it $10,000."

On April 28, Crocker orders eight large Irish men to unload materials. Then you and the other Chinese workers lay the tracks as fast as you can. In 11 hours and 45 minutes, your crew lays more than 10 miles of track. Crocker wins the bet.

Turn the page.

May 10, 1869, is a beautiful day at Promontory Summit, Utah. Two trains from the Central Pacific and two trains from the Union Pacific bring railroad officials and guests. Crocker and Durant are here. So is Stanford Leland, one of the owners of the Central Pacific. Grenville Dodge, the chief engineer of the Union Pacific, is here too.

Special materials have been created for this ceremony. The last railroad tie is made of wood from the California laurel tree. The final railroad spike is made of pure gold.

Just before noon, you and your crew carry one of the last two rails that will join the Central Pacific and the Union Pacific railroads. An Irish crew from the Union Pacific carries the other.

Chinese workers weren't allowed to be in the photos of the golden spike ceremony.

Construction superintendents James Strobridge and Samuel Reed place the laurel tie. Durant sets his spike. Then Stanford places the golden spike. A train car from each side moves forward until they touch. You are part of one of the most important events in American history.

THE END

To follow another path, turn to page 9.
To read the conclusion, turn to page 101.

People sailed from China with little more than the clothes on their backs.

CHAPTER 5

A New Beginning

From 1850 to 1864, the Taiping Rebellion raged in southern China. This civil war left many people without homes and jobs. To survive, they needed to leave China.

California, which the Chinese called Gold Mountain, brought hope. Rumors spread about the gold-filled land. Thousands of Chinese left their country, dreaming of the wealth they would find in the new land.

When the Chinese arrived, there wasn't as much gold as they had been told. Still, there was enough. It just took a little hard work to find. Eventually, many Chinese found gold, but it usually wasn't enough to make them rich.

Other businesses had labor shortages, so Chinese workers had many opportunities. Business owners paid good wages to anyone who would stay in San Francisco and work. Chinese workers built their own area of the city called Chinatown. This part of San Francisco still exists today.

Even more jobs became available during construction of the Transcontinental Railroad. Still searching for gold, most white laborers didn't stay long on the job. In desperation, the company hired thousands of Chinese workers. This move turned out to be a smart one.

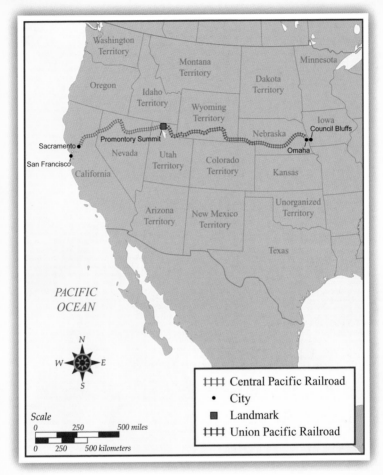

The Chinese worked hard. They laid tracks over flat land. They cut through mountains. They worked through the dry desert. And they completed the track in four years.

For the Chinese, life in America was not always easy. But many succeeded and found a better life than the one they left behind.

They started businesses and introduced Americans to Chinese culture. They opened restaurants that gave Americans their first taste of Chinese food. They invented devices like the water wheel for gold mining and tule shoes for working in the San Joaquin Delta. Most of all, they made major contributions to the United States through their hard work and determination to do well in whatever task was set before them.

Chinese immigrants celebrate their heritage with parades.

TIME LINE

1848 — Gold is discovered at Sutter's Mill near San Francisco.

The ship *American Eagle* brings what may have been the first Chinese immigrants to San Francisco.

1849 — Many more Chinese immigrants arrive in San Francisco. They start building homes and businesses in what will become Chinatown.

1850 — California enacts the first Foreign Miners' Tax, which is repealed the next year.

1852 — California enacts the second Foreign Miners' Tax, aimed at Chinese miners.

106

1862 — The U. S. Congress passes the Pacific Railway Act, which calls for the building of a transcontinental railroad.

1865 — First Chinese workers are hired by the Central Pacific Railroad.

About 50,000 Chinese immigrants live in California.

1866 — The Central Pacific Railroad begins tunnels through the Sierra Nevada mountain range. During that winter, 44 storms hit the mountains.

1867 — White workers form the Anti-Coolie Labor Association in San Francisco. The organization pressures business owners not to hire Chinese workers.

In June, Chinese railroad workers go on strike. Most return to work after one week.

1868 — The Central Pacific Railroad lays tracks through the Nevada desert.

May 10, 1869 — The golden spike ceremony at Promontory Summit, Utah, marks the completion of the Transcontinental Railroad.

July 23, 1877 — A mob burns Chinese-owned businesses in San Francisco.

1882 — The U.S. Congress passes the Chinese Exclusion Act. The law banned Chinese people from immigrating to the United States until 1902. Later acts also restricted Chinese immigration until 1943.

OTHER PATHS TO EXPLORE

In this book, you've seen how the events experienced by Chinese immigrants look different from three points of view.

Perspectives on history are as varied as the people who lived it. You can explore other paths on your own to learn more about what happened. Seeing history from many points of view is an important part of understanding it.

Here are some ideas for other Chinese immigration points of view to explore:

- ✦ Most of the early Chinese immigrants were men who left their families behind. What was it like for these families to stay in a war-torn land?

- ✦ Many white workers saw the hardworking Chinese immigrants as a threat. If you had been a white worker at that time, how would you have felt?

- ✦ Because of racism, most Chinese immigrants settled in areas of big cities that became known as Chinatowns. What would life be like for a Chinese immigrant who decided to live outside of Chinatown?

READ MORE

Anderson, Dale. *Chinese Americans.* Milwaukee: World Almanac Library, 2007.

Behnke, Alison. *Chinese in America.* Minneapolis: Lerner, 2005.

Broida, Marian. *Projects about Nineteenth-Century Chinese Immigrants.* New York: Marshall Cavendish, 2006.

Fine, Jil. *The Transcontinental Railroad: Tracks across America.* New York: Children's Press, 2005.

INTERNET SITES

FactHound offers a safe, fun way to find Internet sites related to this book. All of the sites on FactHound have been researched by our staff.

Here's how:
1. Visit *www.facthound.com*
2. Choose your grade level.
3. Type in this book ID **1429613556** for age-appropriate sites. You may also browse subjects by clicking on letters, or by clicking on pictures and words.
4. Click on the **Fetch It** button.

FactHound will fetch the best sites for you!

GLOSSARY

avalanche (AV-uh-lanch) — a large mass of ice, snow, or earth that suddenly moves down the side of a mountain

grade (GRAYD) — to make more level

hydraulic (hye-DRAW-lik) — power created by liquid being forced under pressure through pipes

immigrant (IM-uh-gruhnt) — a person who leaves one country to live permanently in a new country

Reconstruction (ree-kuhn-STRUHKT-shuhn) — the period of time following the Civil War when the U.S. government tried to rebuild Southern states

sluice (SLOOSS) — a long slanted trough used to mine gold

strike (STRIKE) — to refuse to work because of a disagreement with the employer over wages or working conditions

summit (SUHM-it) — the highest point of a mountain

tule (TOO-lee) — a tall, reedy plant that grows in swampy areas

BIBLIOGRAPHY

Ambrose, Stephen E. *Nothing Like it In the World: The Men Who Built the Transcontinental Railroad 1863–1869.* New York: Simon & Schuster, 2000.

Bain, David Haward. *Empire Express: Building the First Transcontinental Railroad.* New York: Viking, 1999.

Berkeley Digital Library SunSITE
http://sunsite3.berkeley.edu

Brands, H. W. *The Age of Gold: The California Gold Rush and The New American Dream.* New York: Doubleday, 2002.

Central Pacific Railroad Photographic History Museum
http://cprr.org

Chang, Iris. *The Chinese in America: A Narrative History.* New York: Viking, 2003.

A History of Chinese Americans in California: The 1850s
http://www.cr.nps.gov/history/online_books/5views/5views3b.htm

The Virtual Museum of the City of San Francisco
http://www.sfmuseum.org/hist9/cook.html

INDEX